$\mathscr{P}$resente

M000200283

_____

$\mathscr{F}$rom:

_____

$\mathscr{D}$ate:

_____

# HAPPY FATHER'S DAY

*Expressions of Love and Appreciation*
*for the World's Greatest Dad*

## HONOR **HB** BOOKS

*Inspiration and Motivation for the Seasons of Life*

COOK COMMUNICATIONS MINISTRIES,
Colorado Springs, Colorado • Paris, Ontario
KINGSWAY COMMUNICATIONS LTD
Eastbourne, England

Honor Books® is an imprint of
Cook Communications Ministries, Colorado Springs, CO 80918
Cook Communications, Paris, Ontario
Kingsway Communications, Eastbourne, England

Happy Father's Day:
Expressions of Love and Appreciation for the World's Greatest Dad
© 2001 by Honor Books

Printed in the United States of America.

2 3 4 5 6 7 8 9 Printing/Year 10 09 08 07 06

ISBN-13: 978-1-562927-78-3
ISBN-10: 1-56292-778-7

# INTRODUCTION

*H*ey, Dad! This is *your* day! You received this book because someone thought you were too special of a dad for just a card!

In addition to a brief history of Father's Day and interesting Father's Day trivia, this book contains quotes and scriptures that will inspire you; letters from famous people to their parents that might make you cry; stories about dads that will motivate you and make you laugh; quotes from famous people about their dads that will interest you; and poems, greetings, and suggestions on how to have a Happy Father's Day.

You may actually be a dad, or you may be like a dad to someone, but that's the true spirit of Father's Day—honoring those who are fathers in heart, not just through genetics.

May this be your best Father's Day ever!

## NECKTIE TRADITION

*P*erhaps the most notorious Father's Day tradition is the ceremonious (or not so ceremonious) giving of the necktie, complete with its own special box designed to disguise the obvious and most popular gift choice of people who have no idea what to buy their father on his special day.

## DID YOU KNOW?

*T*wo British physicists have solved a knotty problem that men have pondered for more than a hundred years—how to tie the perfect tie.

Using a mathematical model, Thomas Fink and Yong Mao of Cambridge University's Cavendish laboratory produced equations to classify the four most common ways to knot a tie and introduced six new "aesthetically pleasing" knots.

The research, published in the science journal *Nature*, said eighty-five knots could be tied with a conventional tie, but only four—the four-in-hand, the Windsor, the half-Windsor, and the Pratt—were commonly used.[1]

*Nothing I've ever done has
given me more joys and rewards than
being a father to my children.*

—Bill Cosby

*Lo, children* are *an heritage of the* LORD:
and *the fruit of the womb* is his *reward.*

—Psalm 127:3

8

*Life affords no greater responsibility,
no greater privilege, than the
raising of the next generation.*

—C. Everett Koop

## THE GREATEST FAN

*S*everal years ago in a Paris opera house, a famous singer was scheduled to perform, and ticket sales were booming. The night of the concert was a sellout. A rush of excitement and anticipation filled the air as the house manager came to the microphone.

"Ladies and gentlemen, I am sorry I have bad news," he began. "I regret that the singer you've all come to hear will not be performing tonight due to illness. However, I am pleased to present in his absence a young and talented artist who will provide you with a fine evening's entertainment."

The audience groaned in disappointment and sat back to endure the substitute soloist. The stand-in performer gave everything he had, but there was no comparing him with the marquee singer. When he had finished, there was only an uncomfortable silence.

Suddenly, from the balcony a little boy stood up and shouted, "Daddy, I think you are wonderful!"

The crowd broke into thunderous applause.

## A LETTER FROM
## TENNIS STAR
*Tracy Austin to Her Dad*

Dear Dad,

Thank you for spending so much of your free time with me. Although you had a demanding job and five kids, we always felt you were behind us in every way.

I remember you helping me with my homework, especially when I started to travel. You were always patient and willing to help me catch up when I didn't understand something I had missed. I am so glad you stressed the importance of a good education because I'm grateful for it now.

I recall you driving us to tennis tournaments on the weekends and making sure we had the attitude of just doing the best we could. Also, I had a lot of fun when you took my friends and me to the park or horseback riding on Sundays. You and I had a terrific time when we would take long bike rides.

Dad, I want you to know you have been a very good influence and model in shaping my morals and values as a person. Thank you for being such a loving father.[2]

I love you,
Tracy

*B*eing a real father to your children is one job that no one else can ever do as well as you. Good fathers deserve their full share of top praise, for they are helping to build the loftiest cathedrals in the universe—young hearts and minds that are learning how to make this world a better place in which to live.[3]

—John E. Crawford

*N*othing in literature prepares a father for his role. Motherhood is swamped with books—poetic, fictional, factual. No authority discourses on the prenatal and postpartum care of young fathers.

Fatherhood, for me, has been less a job than an unstable and surprising combination of adventure, blindman's bluff, guerrilla warfare, and crossword puzzles.

—Fredrick F. Van de Water

## A TIMELINE OF FATHER'S DAY

1909—Sonora Louise Smart Dodd first conceives the idea for a Father's Day while listening to a Mother's Day sermon.

June 19, 1910—Spokane, Washington, celebrates the first Father's Day.

1924—President Calvin Coolidge supports the idea of a national Father's Day.

1936—National Father's Day Committee is formed.

1957—Senator Margaret Chase Smith tries to persuade Congress to pass a Father's Day proposal.

1966—President Lyndon Johnson signs a presidential proclamation declaring the third Sunday of June as Father's Day.

1972—President Nixon signs a proposal into law making Father's Day a permanent national holiday.

## PATIENCE IS A VIRTUE

*O*ne morning during the usual rush to get the family off to work and school, a father lost his temper and lashed out at his daughter, who just happened to be the closest target. Later that day, when the family was eating supper, Dad tried to make things right.

He began slowly. "I have something I want to talk to you about," he said, looking at everyone but especially eyeing his daughter. "You all know how fast we rush around each morning."

"Uh . . . right," said his daughter.

"Well, I realize I was a little hard to be around this morning," he continued.

Silence.

"I . . . uh . . . want you all to know that I feel bad about it," he said. "And especially, Jane, I'm sorry for what I said to you this morning."

Finally his daughter spoke.

"Dad," she began, "I want you to know that you teach me a lot of things, and I appreciate it."

"Just now," she said, and her face broke into a smile, "you are teaching me patience."

## PASSING THE BATON

[*A* father's] most important responsibility, I believe, is to communicate the real meaning of Christianity to his children. This mission can be likened to a three-man relay race. First, your father runs his lap around the track, carrying the baton, which represents the Gospel of Jesus Christ. At the appropriate moment, he hands the baton to you, and you begin your journey around the track. Then finally, the time will come when you must get the baton safely in the hands of your children. But as any track coach will testify, *relay races are won or lost in the transfer of the baton.*

There is a critical moment when all can be lost by a fumble or miscalculation. The baton is rarely dropped on the back side of the track when the runner has it firmly in his grasp. If failure is to occur, it will probably happen in the exchange between generations.

According to the Christian values that govern my life, my most important reason for living is to get the baton, the Gospel, safely in the hands of my children. . . . I hope millions of other fathers agree with that ultimate priority.[4]

—James Dobson

## HOW TO HAVE A HAPPY FATHER'S DAY

• Spend at least thirty minutes alone with each of your children, focusing all your attention on them individually. You'll be reminded what a great privilege it is to be a father—possibly the best Father's Day gift of all.

- Take your son or daughter out for a first round on the golf course.

- Take your kids for a walk and really talk to them.

*Becoming a father is easy enough,
but being one can be rough.*

—Wilhelm Busch

*Get all the advice you can and be wise the rest of your life.*

—Proverbs 19:20 TLB

24

*B*eing a good father requires knowing when it is an unkindness to your child to let him do as he pleases if what he wants to do is unreasonable or not conducive to happy family living.

—O. Spurgeon English, M.D. and Constance J. Foster

## A LETTER FROM LITERARY GIANT

*Charles Dickens to His Son*

My dearest Plorn,

I put a New Testament among your books . . . with the very same hopes that made me write an easy account of it for you when you were a little child; because it is the best book that ever was or ever will be known in the world, and because it teaches you the best lessons by which any human creature who tries to be truthful and faithful to duty can possibly be guided. As your brothers have gone away, one by one, I have written to each such words as I am now writing to you and entreated them all to guide themselves by this book, putting aside the interpretations and inventions of men. . . .

Only one thing more in this head. The more we are in earnest as to feeling it, the less we are disposed to hold forth about it. Never abandon the wholesome practice of saying your own private prayers, night and morning. I have never abandoned it myself, and I know the comfort of it.

I hope you will always be able to say in after life, that you had a kind father. You cannot show your affection for him so well, or make him so happy, as by doing your duty.[5]

Your affectionate father,
Charles Dickens

# A LETTER FROM COMEDIENNE

*Phyllis Diller to Her Dad*

When Phyllis Diller's dad, Perry Driver, died at the age of eighty-six in 1945, the letter that follows was found folded and dog-eared in his wallet—a clue, perhaps, that a child's words of love and gratitude can mean worlds to a parent at any age.

Dear Dad,

Thank you for all the important things you have given me—a fine education, good genes, and a wonderful secure childhood. You have passed along to me all the best, including a sense of humor. I want you to know how much I appreciate what you have given me.[6]

Love,
Phyllis

## REFLECTIONS OF
## A TRAVELING FATHER

*W*hen television journalist Bob Greene was first asked by others how it felt to be a new father, he recalls, "Normally, I shrug the question off; it's so complicated and so consuming that I don't feel I can do it justice with a glib reply. I usually just say, 'Yeah, it's great,' and let it go at that."

One day, however, he truly expressed to two friends how he felt. He writes in his book, *Good Morning, Merry Sunshine:* "I don't even know how to explain it. I've been spending time on the road ever since I started working for a living. I've complained about it a lot, but I've really liked the idea of it. Going into different cities, sleeping in hotels, meeting strange people . . . I've really liked it.

"Now, though, when I'm gone . . . I physically ache for missing my daughter. It never seems that any story is important enough to make me not see her for another day . . . missing her is not some vague concept in my mind. It actually hurts when I think that she's at home and I'm not with her. Sometimes I fall asleep thinking about it."

*When I was made presidential press secretary my father sent me a telegram: "Always tell the truth. If you can't always tell the truth, don't lie."*

—Bill Moyers

*A good man is known by his truthfulness; a false man by deceit and lies.*

—Proverbs 12:17 TLB

When I was younger, perhaps five or six, one of my biggest thrills was to ask my father to draw something after I went to bed. In the morning I would awake and rush into the living room to find a drawing in his chair. I don't recall any Christmas morning being as exciting as those when I knew there would be a picture waiting for me.

—Russell Chatham

## HOW TO HAVE A HAPPY FATHER'S DAY

- Watch your favorite sports program on TV with your children.

- Explain to your kids why your favorite sport is the "best."

  - Reminisce about the things you did as a child for your own dad on Father's Day.

## DID YOU KNOW?

*T*he simplest necktie knot is the four-in-hand, which originated in the late nineteenth century in England.

The Duke of Windsor, who abdicated the throne in 1936 for the American divorcée Wallis Simpson, is credited with introducing the Windsor knot. The half-Windsor is a simpler version of its predecessor.

The newest knot is the Pratt, which appeared in 1989. The shape of a knot depends on the number of right, center, and left moves in the tie sequence. A balanced knot is tightly bound and keeps its shape.[7]

Dad, thanks for all the time
you've given me over the years.

Your attention and love
mean the world to me.

You are the greatest dad on the planet!

Wisdom, advice,

strength, confidence,

courage, encouragement,

stability, values,

character, integrity,

honesty, sincerity,

Thanks, Dad,
for giving me everything!

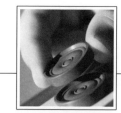

37

*My father was a Methodist and
believed in the laying on of hands,
and believe me, he really laid them on!*

—A.W. Tozer

*Don't fail to correct your children.
They won't die if you spank them. . . .
discipline may well save them from death.*

—Proverbs 23:13–14 NLT

38

*One word of command from me is obeyed by millions . . . but I cannot get my three daughters, Pamela, Felicity, and Joan, to come down to breakfast on time.*

—Viscount Archibald Wavell

## ONCE A FATHER, ALWAYS A FATHER

*T*he main reason why a father's task, no less than a mother's, is the toughest job in the world is that it never ends. . . . Being a parent is a full-time job with no reprieve, no time off even for illness and recuperation. Children, we soon discover, are here to stay for at least a score of years. They don't appear like robins in the spring then fly away at summer's end; or if, as it sometimes seems, they do come and go during high school and college years, their absence in no way lessens our burden of responsibility. In fact, as our children get older, instead of relaxing, our task seemingly intensifies.

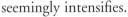

"It's the only job I know," says Ted Hutchens, a father with two daughters still at home and a son away at college, "that never seems to get any easier, in spite of all those years of experience."

. . . The point is clear: Once a parent, always a parent. Fathers and mothers alike, we don't stop caring just because we're no longer the main providers of shelter, food, and the comforts of home. . . . It's also our joyful pleasure to care for them, even after they no longer seem to need us.[8]

—D. Bruce Lockerbie

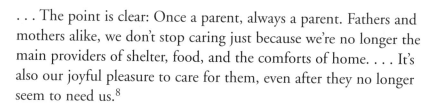

## A LETTER FROM
## GAME-SHOW HOST
*Monty Hall to His Dad*

Dear Dad,

It's three years since you've left us, and with the sale of your condo which was just completed this week, a final curtain has rung down. I remember how you looked forward to our visits to Palm Springs. You asked for our estimated arrival time, and when we drove up, you were always on the front lawn eagerly awaiting us.

In the earlier days, it was both you and Mother; then after her death, you alone—a little more eager, more nervous, as if time were running out and you had so little to spare that each moment we ran behind schedule cheated you of your delicious pleasure with your family.

I know what the visits meant to you, and they were always the same. Questions about my career, my income, my future. Teasing the grandchildren was your favorite sport, but they in return badgered you to give up smoking.

And then all too soon, the weekend was over, the car loaded up and pulled away. You stood in the driveway, smiling and waving—but we knew you had a catch in your throat. You kept asking yourself, "Will there be a next time?" And then—one day, there wasn't. And we all are cheated by time.[9]

Monty

## DADDY

The little child says
Here I am Daddy
As he bursts
On father's sight
From behind the chair
where he's been hiding
He doesn't say
What can I do for you?
How can I help you?
I want to serve you,
Seeking somehow

To work and gain
The father's favor
And delight.
He knows they are his
Without exhausting effort
To achieve.
They are his always.
Here I am Daddy
—Abba Father—
not working
just being
Your eternal son.[10]

—Joseph Bayly

*While I don't minimize the vital role played by a mother, I believe a successful family begins with her husband.*

—James Dobson

He must be *one who manages his own household well, keeping his children under control with all dignity.*

—1 Timothy 3:4 NASB

## MORE FATHER'S DAY HISTORY

*M*rs. John B. Dodd of Washington state first proposed the idea of a "father's day" in 1909. Mrs. Dodd wanted a special day to honor her father, William Smart. William Smart, a Civil War veteran, was widowed when his wife (Mrs. Dodd's mother) died in childbirth with their sixth child. Mr. Smart was left to raise the newborn and his other five children by himself on a rural farm in eastern Washington. It was after Mrs. Dodd became an adult that she realized the strength and selflessness her father had shown in raising his children as a single parent.

## DEVOTION BUILDS A BRIDGE

*T*he Brooklyn Bridge that connects Manhattan and Brooklyn was one of the wonders of the world when it was finished in 1883. Yet it might not have been built were it not for the devotion between a father and his son.

A creative engineer named John Roebling came up with the idea for the unique design, and he put his young son, Washington, in charge of building it. Only a few months into the project, however, a tragic accident took the life of John Roebling and severely injured Washington, who was left unable to walk or talk. It seemed the bridge never would be built, for the Roeblings were the only ones who knew how to do it.

The son's desire to complete the bridge as a tribute to his father drove him with heroic determination. Confined to his hospital bed, he developed a code. With the one finger he could move, he touched his wife's arm, tapping out messages to the construction crew leaders. For the next thirteen years, he communicated his father's vision until it became a spectacular reality.

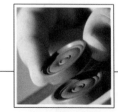

# A LETTER FROM MODELING AGENT

*Eileen Ford to Her Dad*

Dear Dad,

I have been asked to write a letter to you somewhere up in that great Fathers' Place in the sky.

If ever I were to tell you something I have never said, it would be because it is just dawning on me how much I owe you for instilling in me and my brothers a great sense of honesty and responsibility in dealing with others, and, in some way, you got the message through to our four children.

When we meet again, I will thank you in person; but truthfully, I hope that the meeting will not be for a very long time.[11]

Your loving daughter,
Eileen

## A SPECIAL FATHER

*M*arvin Allen tells of meeting Hugh Downs while Downs was taping a special on the men's movement. He writes:

"When I asked Hugh about his dad, his face lit up. He said that he remembered sitting in his dad's lap as a little boy, talking with him for long periods of time. His dad would listen to him and nod thoughtfully, making him feel both wise and worthy of his attention. He talked about the many times his father had taken him to the symphony and explained the names and sounds of the various instruments. He told me of visits to museums and how his dad had discussed art history with him in a way that made it seem fascinating, even to a little boy. As we got to

Hugh's cabin, he said that his father had not only shared a great deal of information with him, he had communicated an overall enthusiasm for life.

"I could see how the joy of the father lived on in the son. Hugh's openness to new ideas, his compassion, and his wide-ranging interests are a testimony to how rich life can be for those fortunate men whose fathers were skilled in the art of dispensing usable love."

*When you are dealing
with a child, keep all your wits
about you and sit on the floor.*

—Austin O'Malley

*God resisteth the proud, and giveth grace to the humble.*

—1 Peter 5:5

## KINGS ARE FATHERS TOO

At the close of the sixteenth century, King Henry IV of France was once interrupted in his royal chamber by the Spanish ambassador. The envoy stood in astonishment at the sight he saw before him. There was the king of France on the floor, playing the part of a horse, while his young son rode atop his back. Although the diplomat was speechless at the sight, the king was matter of fact. "You are a father, too, señor ambassador," he said, "so we will finish our ride."

*By profession I am a soldier*
*and take pride in that fact,*
*but I am prouder to be a father.*

—General Douglas MacArthur

*I have great confidence in you; I take great pride in you.*

—2 Corinthians 7:4 NIV

No man can possibly know what life means, what the world means, what anything means, until he has a child and loves it, and then the whole universe changes, and nothing will ever again seem exactly as it seemed before.

—Lafcadio Hearn

## A GENERAL'S LOVE

*F*ew doubt the bravery and military skill of General Robert E. Lee. As commander of the Army of Northern Virginia, he was known for shrewdness, fast thinking, and an instinct for the counterpunch. He had a keen ability to learn from mistakes and to improvise under the pressure of necessity. Military students still study the way in which he took command and set a course with such mastery that every battle he fought became part of a single campaign.

What many don't know, however, is that Lee had no real taste for war. He much preferred to be at home, romping, playing, and joking with his children, all of whom adored him. The greatest pressure he faced in life was, not leading troops, but in being away from his family. On the day before Christmas 1846, he tenderly wrote: "I hope good Santa Claus will fill my Rob's stocking tonight; that Mildred's, Agnes's, and Anna's may break down with good things . . . but if he only leaves for you one-half of what I wish, you will want for nothing."

## A FATHER'S FAITH

*M*artin Luther once wrote this about the role of a husband and father:

"Along comes the clever harlot, namely natural reason, looks at married life, turns up her nose and says: 'Why must I rock the baby, wash its diapers, change its bed, smell its odor, heal its rash, take care of this and take care of that, do this and do that? It is better to remain single and live a quiet and carefree life. I will become a priest or a nun and tell my children to do the same.'

"But what does the Christian faith say? The father opens his eyes, looks at these lowly, distasteful, and despised things and knows that they are adorned with divine approval as with the most precious gold and silver. God, with His angels and creatures, will smile—not because diapers are washed, but because it is done in faith."

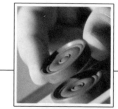

*Like father, like son:*
*every good tree maketh good fruits.*

—William Langland

*"Even so every good tree bringeth forth good fruit."*

—Matthew 7:17

It is a delight above all delights to see one's children turn out—as ours have done—all that the heart covets in children; and my delight is so full that I sometimes fancy my heart will have to burst for its own relief.

—Henry James Sr.

## THE BEST PRESENT EVER

*W*hile a grown man was awaiting surgery in a hospital, he began talking with his father. The two recalled various Father's Day celebrations they had shared through the years, and then the son said wistfully, "I still feel awful that when I was ten years old, I didn't give you either a card or a gift."

The father replied, "Son, I remember the Saturday before that Father's Day. I saw you in a store, although you didn't see me. I watched as you picked up several cigars and stuffed them into your pocket. I knew you had no money, and I suspected you were about to steal those cigars as a present for me. I felt extremely sad to think you would leave the store without

64

paying for them. But almost as soon as you tucked the cigars into your pocket, you pulled them out and put them back into the box on the shelf.

"When you stayed out playing all the next day because you had no present to give me, you probably thought I was hurt. You were wrong. When you put those cigars back and decided not to break the law, you gave me the best Father's Day present I ever received."

# A LETTER FROM PRESIDENT

*George Bush to His Dad*

Dear Dad,

It is hard sometimes for a man to say this to another man; but I love you very much—always have, always will—[12]

George

*You don't need to be right all the time.*
*Your child wants a man for a father, not a formula.*
*He wants real parents, real people, capable of*
*making mistakes without moping about it.*

—C.D. Williams

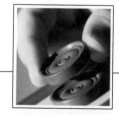

## HERSHISER'S GREATEST ROLE MODEL

*P*itching great Orel Hershiser is often regarded as a role model for young people. But who was his primary role model? In his book *Out of the Blue*, Hershiser describes his role model as a man who was very competitive yet generous and a gentleman. "In everything he does," says Hershiser, "he wants to win. . . . Sometimes he would compete only with himself. I saw that side of him even in how he cleaned the garage. He took care of every detail and put everything in its place.

"He always commended and rewarded those who did a good job. A perfectionist, he often demanded that a job be done repeatedly, but even so, he gave a pat on the back in encouragement. He didn't mind pain, and he didn't mind work. And he had a grand habit of asking 'Why?' When others might say in the face of a weather prediction of rain, 'There goes our golf date tomorrow,' he would say, 'Why? Does the weatherman have to be right? We don't know what tomorrow will be like. The storm may pass through. Let's plan on playing and see if it works out.' He was a stubborn optimist with a never-give-up attitude."

Who was this superlative role model? His dad!

## HAPPY FATHER'S DAY

*D*ad, I don't tell you often enough,
but I appreciate the man that you are—
someone who stands up for what he believes
even in the face of opposition.

I thank God every morning
that He's given me a father like you
to remind me of the Father that He is.

—B.J. Reardon

*There is no more vital calling
or vocation for men than fathering.*

—John R. Throop

*I press toward the mark for the prize
of the high calling of God in Christ Jesus.*

—Philippians 3:14

*M*en cannot be developed perfectly who have not been compelled to bring children up to manhood. You might as well say that a tree is a perfect tree without leaf or blossom, as to say that a man is a man who has gone through life without experiencing the influences that come from bending down and giving one's self up to those who are helpless and little.

—Henry Ward Beecher

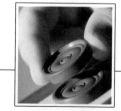

*A* father once found this note pinned to the bulletin board by the family phone:

Daddy—I am going to wash my hair. If Tom calls, tell him to call at 8:00. If Herb calls and Tom doesn't, tell Herb to call at 8:00, but if they both call, tell Herb to call at 8:15 or 8:30. If Timmy calls and Tom and Herb don't, tell Timmy to call at 8:00, but if they both call (Tom & Herb) or one calls, tell Timmy to call at 8:30 or 8:40—Tina

*Father:*
*A man who can't get on the phone,*
*into the bathroom, or out of the house.*

*There is a right time for everything: . . . A time to laugh.*

—Ecclesiastes 3:1,4 TLB

*A father's words are like a thermostat that sets the temperature in the house.*

—Paul Lewis

*By the time a man realizes
that maybe his father was right,
he usually has a son who thinks he's wrong.*

—Charles Wadworth

## GRAND OLE' OPRY STAR

*Minnie Pearl's Letter to Her Dad*

Dear Daddy,

You never knew how much I loved you. I told you, I'm sure, but never in the right way—nor enough.

Thank you for so many things. For making me aware of beauty in nature; for teaching me bird calls when I was a tot; for teaching me to love to read; for teaching me to respect the dignity of others, regardless of creed, race, or color; for sharing your wonderful sense of humor; for teaching me to be proud of my country "raisin"; and for teaching me to tell the truth (the hard way, by catching me in a lie!).

Most of all though, Daddy, you taught me to love God and the Golden Rule. You lived by that and taught all of your children by example rather than words.

I still miss you, Daddy. I could go on and on. I still love you devotedly.[13]

Sara Opehlia Colley Cannon
(Minnie Pearl)

## DON'T WORRY

*A* recollection by pastor-author James S. Hewitt:

"When I was a small boy growing up in Pennsylvania, often we would visit my grandparents who lived nine miles away. One night a thick fog settled over the hilly countryside before we started home. I remember being terrified and asking if we shouldn't be going slower than we were. Mother said gently, 'Don't worry. Your father knows the way.'

"You see, my dad had walked that road when there was no gasoline during the war. He had ridden that blacktop on his bicycle to court Mother. And for years he had made those weekly trips back to visit his own parents.

"How often when I can't see the road ahead, and that feeling of being lost has returned, I hear the echo of my mother's voice: 'Don't worry. Your Father knows the way.'"

## FATHER AND SON

$\mathcal{D}$onald Grey Barnhouse has written a brief essay on "Father and Son," in which he says,

"If a man begets a son, in consequence of that act, he is always the father of that son. There have been men who have been fathers 'of' sons who have never been fathers 'to' their sons. But many a man who begets a child gives himself to that child. He is with the mother in the training of the child. The boy is with the father in his free moments.

"The father enters into the boy's studies; he participates in the boy's games. He makes the boy's hobbies his own hobbies. No question the boy is beyond the patience of the father. He explains things to the child in great detail whenever the child shows interest in an answer. He trains the boy, leads him on, truly educates him. It can be said in the highest degree that this man is, not only father 'of' the boy, he is father 'to' the boy."

*Dad, when you come home at night with only shattered pieces of your dreams, your little one can mend them like new with two magic words——— "Hi, Dad!"*

—Alan Beck

*We have great joy and consolation in thy love.*

—Philemon 1:7

*I sigh that I kiss you, for I must own
that I shall miss you when you have grown.*

—William Butler Yeats

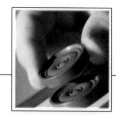

## A BLUE-RIBBON DAD

*A* proud father looked at the blue ribbon on the paper before him and began to read what his daughter had written: "We called him 'Daddy' when we were young. He was able to make even folding clothes on Saturday fun, with tickle fights amidst freshly washed garments strewn all over the living-room floor. He would roll and pretend at vulnerability on the carpet and grab each tiny, groping hand that attempted to tweak his ribs. We seldom won, of course. Daddy could mercilessly tickle. . . .

"There were serious times as well. He could spank the tears out of any of us, not because the physical pain was so incredible, but because it hurt us to think that we had brought him pain by having earned that spanking.

"High moral values, spiritual priorities, academic excellence—all these have been held out to us as important. My pop has instilled in us kids a sense of trust. He's been available, especially in emergencies. He has done what he thinks best for us, even when we might not agree. . . . My dad has a corner on the upper echelons of fatherhood."

## A LETTER FROM COUNTRY SINGER

*Loretta Lynn to Her Dad*

Dear Daddy,

You know, we've always been a close family, but we never said much about it. I wish I had told you how much I love you. I just took it for granted that you knew. But ever since you've been gone, I make it a point to tell all of the family how much I love them anytime we're together and have to part again.

I also wish you could have lived to see me sing. You always believed in me, and I guess you were right.[14]

I miss you more than ever, Daddy.

Loretta

*I* was a shy, solemn child even at the age of two, and I am sure that even when I danced, I never smiled. My earliest recollections are of being dressed up and allowed to come down to dance for a group of gentleman who applauded and laughed as I pirouetted before them. Finally, my father would pick me up and hold me high in the air. He dominated my life as long as he lived and was the love of my life for many years after he died.[15]

—Eleanor Roosevelt

## A FATHER'S GIFT

*A*uthor Phyllis Theroux writes about how her father helped her deal with failure:

"If there was any one thing my father did for me when I was growing up, it was to give me the promise that ahead of me was dry land—a bright, marshless territory, without chuckholes or traps, where one day I would walk easily and as befitting my talents. . . .

"Thus it was, when he came upon me one afternoon sobbing out my unsuccesses into a wet pillow, that he sat down on the bed and assured me that my grief was only a temporary setback. Oh, very temporary! Why, he couldn't think of any other little girl who was so talented, so predestined to succeed in every department as I was.

'And don't forget,' he added with a smile, 'that we can trace our ancestry right back to Pepin the Stupid!'

"There are some people who carry the flint that lights other people's torches. . . . That was my father's gift to me."

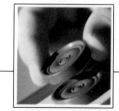

*My father is the standard
by which all subsequent men
in my life have been judged.*

—Kathryn McCarthy Graham

*Leaving us an example, that ye should follow his steps.*

—1 Peter 2:21

*To an old father, nothing is more sweet than a daughter. Boys are more spirited, but their ways are not so tender.*

—Euripides

*My father taught me how to deal
with overly male men: don't react,
just say yes, and don't pay any attention.*

—Katharine Hepburn

## A FATHER'S INFLUENCE

"*B*e home by midnight or . . . sleep on the porch."

By the age of fourteen, Oprah Gail Winfrey was headed for trouble. She stayed out late or didn't come home at all and hung around with a fast crowd. Her desperate mother persuaded Oprah's father, Vernon Winfrey, a barbershop owner, to take her. In the first "real home" she had ever known, Oprah learned about curfews, discipline, hard work, and good grades. Today Oprah says, "My father turned my life around by insisting I be more than I was and by believing I could be more."[16]

## A PRAYER OF SURRENDER

*M*artin Luther had a reputation as an excellent father who had just the right way with discipline and love. He believed: "Punish if you must, but let the sugarplum go with the rod." He composed songs for his children, playing his lute while his children sang them. His letters to his children are jewels.

Luther especially had a tender place in his heart for his daughter, Magdalena, about whom he said, "God has given no bishop so great a gift in a thousand years as He has given me in her." When she became ill at the age of fourteen, he prayed constantly for her, finally praying:

"I love her very much, but, dear God, if it is Thy holy will to take her, I would gladly leave her with Thee." To Lena he said, "Dear, my little daughter, thou wouldst love to remain here with thy father; art thou willing to go to that other Father?" His daughter said, "Yes, dear Father, just as God wills." When she died, he wept long, and as she was laid in the earth, he spoke to her as to a living soul: "You will rise and shine like the stars and the sun."

May all fathers see their children as far more valuable than the riches of this earth.

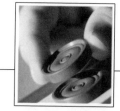

*My dad and I hunted and fished together.*
*How could I get angry at this man*
*who took the time to be with me?*

—James Dobson

*Honour thy father.*

—Exodus 20:12

*We never know the love of the parent until we become parents ourselves.*

—Henry Ward Beecher

*To understand your parents' love, you must raise children yourself.*

—Chinese Proverb

## A TRUE STORY

*D*avid Elkind, the famous child psychologist and author of the best-selling book *The Hurried Child* tells this true story about his role as a parent:

"I remember visiting my middle son's nursery school class, at the request of his teacher, so that I could observe a 'problem child' in the class. It so happened that I was sitting and observing a group of boys, including my son, who sat in a circle nearby.

"Their conversation went like this:

"Child A: 'My daddy is a doctor, and he makes a lot of money, and we have a swimming pool.'

"Child B: 'My daddy is a lawyer, and he flies to Washington and talks to the president.'

"Child C: 'My daddy owns a company, and we have our own airplane.'

"Then my son (with aplomb, of course): 'My daddy is here!'"

## THE RIGHT DECISION

*T*he two boys were dressed and ready to go. Excitement flooded their faces, and all their talk was about only one thing: their father had promised to take them to the circus that afternoon!

As planned, Dad came home from work after lunch and quickly changed into casual clothing. Then, just as the three of them were about to leave the house, the phone rang. The boys listened as their father talked with the person on the other end of the line. This was obviously a business call, and some urgent matter was requiring their father's attention downtown. Disappointment rolled into the room like a dark cloud.

Their mother also overheard what she thought was the inevitable change of plans. And then, to the surprise of all, they heard Dad say, "No, I won't be down. It will just have to wait until morning."

Hanging up the phone, he called for the boys to meet him at the car as he turned to kiss his wife good-bye. She smiled and with a twinge of fear that he may have made the wrong decision, she said, "The circus keeps coming back, you know."

The father replied, "Yes, I know. But childhood doesn't."

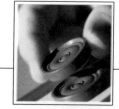

*Authentic men aren't afraid to show affection, release their feelings, hug their children, cry when they're sad, admit it when they're wrong, and ask for help when they need it.*

—Charles Swindoll

*My dad and I once went down to Taxco, Mexico, for the purpose of reading aloud to each other G.K. Chesterton's Orthodoxy.*

—Christopher Buckley of his father, William F. Buckley Jr.

*I*f you're a dad, what kind of mark are you leaving on your children, especially your sons? Do you realize that your little boys are watching you like hawks? They're trying to figure out what maleness is all about, and you're their model. I hope they see in you a deep, uncompromising love for God. I hope they see both toughness and tenderness. If they do, then you have served them well; they will be forever grateful. Your little girls, too, will benefit because they'll grow up with a clear vision of the kind of men who make Godly husbands.[17]

—Bill Hybels

## MORE FATHER'S DAY HISTORY

After conceiving her idea in 1909, Mrs. Dodd drew up a petition recommending adoption of a national Father's Day. The Spokane Ministerial Association and the local Young Men's Christian Association supported it. Through Dodd's efforts, Spokane celebrated the first Father's Day on June 19, 1910. In the ensuing years, many resolutions to make the day an official national holiday were introduced, but it wasn't until 1972 that President Nixon signed into law a proposal to make Father's Day a permanent national observance on the third Sunday of June.[18]

## A FUN KIND OF DAD

*A* family once planned a month's vacation to the West Coast. At the last minute, the father was unable to go because of work responsibilities. Mom insisted she was capable of driving, and she and the children went ahead with their trip. Dad helped plan their route and arranged where they would stop each night.

As it turned out, Dad was able to complete his work within two weeks. He decided to surprise the family, so he flew to a West Coast city without calling them. Then he took a taxi out of the city and asked to be let off along the highway on which, according to his travel plan, the family should be driving later that day. When he saw the family car, he stuck out his thumb. As Mom and the children drove past, they did a double take.

"Mom, wasn't that Dad?"

The car came to a screeching hault, and the family enjoyed a joyful reunion.

When a reporter later asked the man why he did such a crazy thing, he said, "After I die, I want my kids to be able to say, 'Dad sure was fun, wasn't he!'"

## A Father's Influence

*T*he late TV lecturer and best-selling author Leo Buscaglia often said this about the guidance he received from his father:

"Papa believed that the greatest sin was to go to bed at night as ignorant as when we awakened.

"Papa insisted that each child learn one new thing each day. Dinnertime was the forum for sharing new facts and insights. At the end of the meal came the question asked solemnly of each child, 'Tell me what you learned today.' Before the meal was over, the entire family had been enlightened by at least half a dozen facts.

"The news we recounted, no matter how insignificant, was never taken lightly. Mama and Papa listened carefully and were ready with some comment, often profound and analytical, always to the point.

"In retrospect, I realize what a dynamic educational technique Papa was offering us. Without being aware of it, our family was growing together, sharing experiences, and participating in one another's education. And by listening to us, respecting our input, affirming our value, and giving us a sense of dignity, Papa unquestionably was our most influential teacher."

## A PARENT'S PRAYER

*F*ather, we need reminders. I need reminders. And so we are thankful for the reminders You give us daily in the form of our children. Reminders, first, of Your generosity, for children are a gift from You. But reminders, as well, of our finitude, or our place in this world that You have created. Reminders that we are stewards of Your creation, not its gods. Reminders that we tend the seeds that You have sown, but we do

not determine the plant's growth. Reminders that our final duty is to honor You through our acts of service to one another, not to serve and honor ourselves. *May God grant us the wisdom to be parents whose treasure lies in heaven and not in the applause of others.*[19]

—S.D. Gaede

## MORE FATHER'S DAY HISTORY

$\mathcal{I}$n 1936, a national Father's Day Committee was formed, with headquarters in New York City. The Father of the Year is elected annually. Among men chosen have been Douglas MacArthur, Ralph J. Bunche, Dwight D. Eisenhower, and Harry S Truman.

*Measure wealth, not by the things you have, but by the things you have for which you would not take money.*

—Anonymous

*"A man's life does not consist in the abundance of his possessions."*

—Luke 12:15 NIV

To be sure, working—that is, earning a living—is one aspect of fathering. It's one means that the father has of extending protection to his family, but it's just one. If he concentrates on this to the exclusion of other aspects, it becomes not a form of fathering, but an escape.

—Myron Brenton

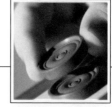

*Fathering is a marathon, not a sprint.*

—Paul L. Lewis

*Let us run with patience the race that is set before us.*

—Hebrews 12:1

*T*he acid test of a father's leadership is not in the realm of his social skills, his public relations, his managerial abilities at the office, or how well he handles himself before the public. It is in the home.

—Charles Swindoll

## A LETTER FROM ROCKEFELLER'S SON

*S*hortly before his ninety-fourth birthday, John D. Rockefeller received this letter from his son:

"I have tried to do what I thought you would have me do. . . . I have endeavored to use wisely and unselfishly the means that you have unselfishly placed at my disposal. . . . In all these years of effort and

striving, your own life and example have ever been to me the most powerful and stimulating influence. What you have done for humanity and business on a vast scale has impressed me profoundly. To have been a silent partner with you in carrying out these great constructive purposes and benefactions has been the supreme delight of my life."

*Norman Schwarzkopf described him as a "true patriot." Michael Jordan said he was "my best friend." F. Scott Fitzgerald may have said it most simply——"I love my father."* [20]

—Dave and Elsa Hornfischer

*He shall turn the heart of the fathers to the children, and the heart of the children to their fathers.*

—Malachi 4:6

## GROWING UP

*B*ill Cosby writes in *Fatherhood*, "Some authority on parenting once said, 'Hold them very close and then let them go.' This is the hardest truth for a father to learn: that his children are continuously growing up and moving away from him (until, of course, they move back in). Such growth is especially bittersweet with a daughter because you are always in love with her."

When rejection by a daughter occurs, Cosby advises, "You have to remember that it means no lessening of her love. You must use this rejection to prepare yourself for others that will be coming, like the one I received on a certain day when I called my daughter at college. Someone in her dorm picked up the phone, and I asked to speak to my daughter. The person left and returned about a minute later to say, 'She says she's sleeping right now.'

"I was hurt to have my daughter put me on hold, but intellectually I knew that this was just another stage in her growth; and I remembered what Spencer Tracy had said in *Father of the Bride:* 'Your son is your son till he takes him a wife, but your daughter is your daughter for all of your life.' "

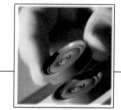

*When these parenting years have passed, something precious will have flickered and gone out of my life. Thus, I am resolved to enjoy every day that remains in this fathering era.*

—James Dobson

*There is a time for everything, and a season for every activity under heaven.*

—Ecclesiastes 3:1 NIV

*Don't be discouraged if your children reject your advice. Years later they will offer it to their own offspring.*

*A man ought to live so that everybody knows he is a Christian . . . and most of all, his family ought to know.*

—D.L. Moody

*Fathers, do not exasperate your children; instead, bring them up in the training and instruction of the Lord.*

—Ephesians 6:4 NIV

124

*I* strive to be as careful and gentle with my son as my father was with his. I am trying very hard to be these things because I understand that what I say and do will live with him long beyond my time, just as what my father said and did survived his time. And though I know we are different, I am grateful for what I have of my father in me. It is my gift, my promise to myself and my children.

—Kenneth Barrett

*It takes time to be a good father.*
*It takes effort——————trying,*
*failing, and trying again.*

—Tim Hansel

*Let us not get tired of doing what is right,*
*for after a while we will reap a harvest of*
*blessing if we don't get discouraged and give up.*

—Galatians 6:9 TLB

There are to us no ties at all just in being a father. A son is distinctly an acquired taste. It's the practice of parenthood that makes you feel that, after all, there may be something in it.

—Heywood Broun

## ONE FATHER'S METHOD

*I*n their classic book *Cheaper by the Dozen*, Frank B. Gilbreth Jr. and Ernestine Gilbreth Carey describe their father as a man who "always practiced what he preached, and it was just about impossible to tell where his scientific management company ended and his family life began. His office was always full of children, and he often took two or three of us, and sometimes all twelve, on business trips. . . .

"On the other hand, our house at Montclair, New Jersey, was a sort of school for scientific management and the elimination of wasted motions."

Gilbreth installed work charts in the bathrooms, took moving pictures of his children doing chores to help identify wasted motion, and insisted that a child who wanted extra pocket money submit a sealed bid, with the lowest bidder getting the contract. Still, his children didn't seem to mind their regimented life. Why? Primarily because "he had a respect for them, too, and didn't mind showing it." He believed about children that "there's no limit to what you can teach. Really, it was a love of children more than anything else that made him want a pack of his own."

*Some fathers bring up their children on thunder and lightning, but thunder and lightning never yet made anything grow.*

*You should practice tenderhearted mercy and kindness to others. . . . Most of all, let love guide your life.*

—Colossians 3:12,14 TLB

*One father is worth more
than a hundred schoolmasters.*

—George Herbert

*I owe almost everything to my father.*

—Margaret Thatcher

*Honour thy father . . . as the LORD*
*thy God hath commanded thee.*

—Deuteronomy 5:16

132

*Life's journey is circular it appears.
The years don't carry us away from
our fathers——they return us to them.*

—Michel Marriott

*B*orn into a world of wealth, but awkward and plain as a child, Eleanor Roosevelt treasured her father's attention. Elliot Roosevelt regularly wrote his daughter words of devotion and encouragement like these:

"The next time you are walking, go by a house that is being built. Watch the workmen bring one stone after another and place it on the one gone before. Then think there are a lot of funny little workmen running about in your small golden head called 'Ideas,' which are carrying a lot of stones like 'Facts. . . .' These 'Fact Stones' . . . build a beautiful house called 'Education.'"

In 1951, Eleanor said of her father, "He lives in my dreams to this day."[21]

*Papa: A fond name for father, used in many languages.*

*Fatherly: Paternal; like a father; tender; protecting; careful.*

*Fatherliness: The tenderness of a father; paternal kindness.*

—Samuel Johnson

*When I was a boy of fourteen,*
*my father was so ignorant I could*
*hardly stand to have the old man around.*
*But when I got to be twenty-one,*
*I was astonished at how much*
*the old man had learned.*

—Mark Twain

*Honor your father and mother.*

—Ephesians 6:2 NIV

*Insanity is hereditary:
you can get it from your children.*

—Samuel Levenson

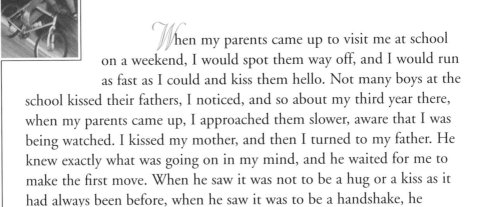

When my parents came up to visit me at school on a weekend, I would spot them way off, and I would run as fast as I could and kiss them hello. Not many boys at the school kissed their fathers, I noticed, and so about my third year there, when my parents came up, I approached them slower, aware that I was being watched. I kissed my mother, and then I turned to my father. He knew exactly what was going on in my mind, and he waited for me to make the first move. When he saw it was not to be a hug or a kiss as it had always been before, when he saw it was to be a handshake, he smiled and put out his hand to meet mine.

—Philip B. Kunhardt Jr.

$\mathcal{I}$ think of him as being very affectionate, but I don't remember him putting his arm around me. You always had the sense that he had great feeling for you. You saw him providing for you, at enormous pain to himself. You saw him doing nothing for himself—never bought himself anything, never enjoyed himself . . . so the overwhelming impression we got was that this man was offering us his life; he didn't have to put his arm around you.[22]

—Mario Cuomo

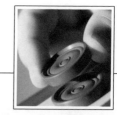

## MORE FATHER'S DAY HISTORY

*I*n 1957, Senator Margaret Chase Smith tried to persuade Congress to give dads their own special day. When that didn't work, she tried to shame them into it with a strongly worded statement: "As far as I can gather, it seems that the Congress has been guilty now for forty years of the worst possible oversight, to say the least, perpetrated against the gallant fathers, young and old, of our land. . . . Either we honor both parents, mother and father, or let us desist from honoring either one. But to single out just one of our two parents and omit the other is the most grievous insult imaginable."

Even though Senator Smith's point seems obvious today, it didn't sway the Congress; they still refused to give fathers their day.

*I believe the family was established long before the church, and my duty is to my family first. I am not to neglect my family.*

—D.L. Moody

*If any provide not for his own, and specially for those of his own house, he hath denied the faith, and is worse than an infidel.*

—1 Timothy 5:8

We think of a father as an old, or at least a middle-aged man. The astounding truth is that most fathers are young men, and that they make their greatest sacrifices in their youth. I never meet a young man in a public park on Sunday morning wheeling his first baby in a perambulator without feeling an ache of reverence.

—James Douglas

*A father who teaches his children responsibility provides them with a fortune.*

*A father is a banker
provided by nature.*

—French Proverb

*I can remember playing under the big wooden
desk in his office. My mother didn't like us
to chew gum, so we'd go into his office, and
he'd feed us gum under the desk.*

—John F. Kennedy Jr.

144

*Can't you see the Creator of the universe, who understands every secret, every mystery . . . sitting patiently and listening to a four-year-old talk to Him? That's a beautiful image of a father.*

—James Dobson

145

*My daddy doesn't work;*
*he just goes to the office, but sometimes*
*he does errands on the way home.*

—from *Ladies Home Journal*, November 1946

## A FATHER'S LEGACY

*J*ohann Sebastian Bach doted on his talented son, taught him everything he knew, and rejoiced in Johann Christian's devotion to the discipline he loved so much. "I can arrange a fine concert with voices and instruments, using only members of my family," he said.

After his father's death, fifteen-year-old Johann Christian learned that his father had willed him three of his favorite instruments. Shortly thereafter, he left Leipzig, taking with him, not only the instruments, but also, according to his biographer, "a solid technical foundation and musical heritage no other young musician of his day could call his own."[23]

*The time not to become a father is eighteen years before a world war.*

—E.B. White

*If your children want to alter society, listen to their reasons and the idealism behind them. Don't crush them with some clever remark straight away.*

—Prince Charles

*M*y father was a true father—he loved me. And because he loved me, I loved him: first, as a child, with the love which is worship; then, as a youth, with the love that vies battle; last, as a man, with the love which understands.

—e.e. cummings

It's a wonderful feeling when your father becomes, not a god, but a man to you—when he comes down from the mountain, and you see he's this man with weakness. And you love him as this whole being, not as a figurehead.

—Robin Williams

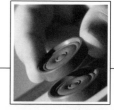

*When children sound silly, you will always find that it is in imitation of their elders.*

—Ernest Dimnet

*Be imitators of God, as beloved children; and walk in love, just as Christ also loved you.*

—Ephesians 5:1–2 NASB

*The way it is in our family, we try
to make something happen rather
than waiting for it to happen.*

—Michael Jordan

Just as his game was coming around, Michael Jordan found himself on academic suspension from high school. But he wasn't quick to catch the implications of his failure. When his father, James, asked him about his goals, Michael mentioned playing college basketball. "How can you make it to college," his father asked, "if you are not going to graduate from high school?"

Good question.[24]

## DAD

*If* he's wealthy and prominent, and you stand in awe of him, call him "Father." If he sits in his shirt sleeves and suspenders at a ball game and picnic, call him "Pop." If he wheels the baby carriage and carries bundles meekly, call him "Papa" (with the accent on the first syllable). If he belongs to a literary circle and writes cultured papers, call him "Papa" (with the accent on the last syllable).

*If,* however, he makes a pal of you when you're good and is too wise to let you pull the wool over his loving eyes when you're not; if, moreover, you're quite sure no other fellow you know has quite so fine a father, you may call him "Dad."

—William Buel Franklin

# REFERENCES

Unless otherwise indicated, all Scripture quotations are taken from the *King James Version* of the Bible.

Verses marked TLB are taken from *The Living Bible* © 1971. Used by permission of Tyndale House Publishers, Inc., Wheaton, Ilinois 60189. All rights reserved.

Scripture quotations marked NASB are taken from the *New American Standard Bible*. Copyright © The Lockman Foundation 1960, 1962, 1963, 1968, 1971, 1972, 1973, 1975, 1977, 1995, 1997. Used by permission.

Scripture quotations marked NIV are taken from the *Holy Bible, New International Version* ®. NIV ®. Copyright © 1973, 1978, 1984 by International Bible Society. Used by permission of Zondervan Publishing House. All rights reserved.

Scripture quotations marked NLT is taken from the *Holy Bible, New Living Translation*, copyright © 1996. Used by permission of Tyndale House Publishers, Inc., Wheaton, Illinois 60189. All rights reserved.

# Endnotes

1 (p. 7) Patricia Reaney, "Physicists Tie One On," *Reuters* (March 4, 1999).

2 (p. 13) L. Norma Cox, ed., *Dear Dad: Famous People's Loving Letters to Their Fathers* (New York, NY: Saybrook Publishing Company, 1987) p. 9.

3 (p. 14) John Crawford, *Being the Real Father Now that Your Teenager Will Need* (Fortress Press, 1968) as quoted in the *Men's Devotional Bible* (Grand Rapids, MI: Zondervan Publishing, 1993) p. 1347.

4 (p. 21) James Dobson, *Straight Talk to Men and Their Wives* (Dallas, TX: Word, Inc., 1980) as quoted in the *Men's Devotional Bible* (Grand Rapids, MI: Zondervan Publishing, 1993) p. 595.

5 (p. 27) *Father of My Heart* (New York, NY: Hearst Books, 1996) p. 65.

6 (p. 29) L. Norma Cox, ed., *Dear Dad: Famous People's Loving Letters to Their Fathers* (New York, NY: Saybrook Publishing Company, 1987) pp. 56, 58.

7 (p. 35) Patricia Reaney, "Physicists Tie One On," *Reuters* (March 4, 1999).

8 (p. 41) D. Bruce Lockerbie, *Fatherlove* (Doubleday, 1981) as quoted in the *Men's Devotional Bible* (Grand Rapids, MI: Zondervan Publishing, 1993) p. 1259.

9 (p. 43) L. Norma Cox, ed., *Dear Dad: Famous People's Loving Letters to Their Fathers* (New York, NY: Saybrook Publishing Company, 1987) pp. 70–71.

10 (p. 45) Joseph Bayly, *Psalms of My Life* (David C. Cook Publishing Co.) as quoted in the *Men's Devotional Bible* (Grand Rapids, MI: Zondervan Publishing, 1993) p. 1325.

11 (p. 51) L. Norma Cox, ed., *Dear Dad: Famous People's Loving Letters to Their Fathers* (New York, NY: Saybrook Publishing Company, 1987) p. 61.

12 (p. 66) L. Norma Cox, ed., *Dear Dad: Famous People's Loving Letters to Their Fathers* (New York, NY: Saybrook Publishing Company, 1987) p. 34.

13 (p. 79) L. Norma Cox, ed., *Dear Dad: Famous People's Loving Letters to Their Fathers* (New York, NY: Saybrook Publishing Company, 1987) p. 106.

[14] (p. 88) L. Norma Cox, ed., *Dear Dad: Famous People's Loving Letters to Their Fathers* (New York, NY: Saybrook Publishing Company, 1987) p. 89.

[15] (p. 89) L. Norma Cox, ed., *Dear Dad: Famous People's Loving Letters to Their Fathers* (New York, NY: Saybrook Publishing Company, 1987) p. 147.

[16] (p. 95) Dave and Elsa Hornfischer, *Father Knew Best: Wit and Wisdom from the Dads of Celebrities* (New York, NY: Dutton, 1997).

[17] (p. 106) Bill Hybels, *Honest to God?* (Grand Rapids, MI: Zondervan Publishing, 1990) as quoted in the *Men's Devotional Bible* (Grand Rapids, MI: Zondervan Publishing, 1993) p. 805.

[18] (p. 107) *www.chron.com/content/interactive/special/holidays/97/dad/history.html*

[19] (p. 112) S.D. Gaede, *Life in the Slow Lane* (Grand Rapids, MI: Zondervan) as quoted in the *Men's Devotional Bible* (Grand Rapids, MI: Zondervan Publishing, 1993) p. 1140.

[20] (p. 119) Dave and Elsa Hornfischer, *Father Knew Best: Wit and Wisdom from the Dads of Celebrities* (New York, NY: Dutton, 1997).

[21] (p. 134) Dave and Elsa Hornfischer, *Father Knew Best: Wit and Wisdom from the Dads of Celebrities* (New York, NY: Dutton, 1997).

[22] (p. 139) L. Norma Cox, ed., *Dear Dad: Famous People's Loving Letters to Their Fathers* (New York, NY: Saybrook Publishing Company, 1987) p. 151.

[23] (p. 147) Dave and Elsa Hornfischer, *Father Knew Best: Wit and Wisdom from the Dads of Celebrities* (New York, NY: Dutton, 1997).

[24] (p. 153) Dave and Elsa Hornfischer, *Father Knew Best: Wit and Wisdom from the Dads of Celebrities* (New York, NY: Dutton, 1997).

Additional copies of this and other
titles from Honor Books are available
wherever good books are sold.

v v v

If you have enjoyed this book,
or if it has had an impact on your life,
we would like to hear from you.

Please contact us at:

HONOR BOOKS
Cook Communications Ministries, Dept. 201
4050 Lee Vance View
Colorado Springs, CO 80918

Or visit our Web site:
www.cookministries.com

# HONOR ⬛ BOOKS
*Inspiration and Motivation for the Seasons of Life*